Social Anxiety

Easy Daily Strategies for Overcoming Social Anxiety and Shyness, Build Successful Relationships and Increase Happiness

By

James W. Williams

Table of Contents

Your Free Gift

As a way of saying thanks for your purchase, I wanted to offer you a free bonus E-book called *"Bulletproof Confidence Checklist: Eliminate Limiting Beliefs, Overcome Shyness and Social Anxiety and Achieve Your Goals"*.

In this guide, you will discover:

- What is shyness & social anxiety and the psychology behind it
- Simple treatments for social anxiety
- Breakdown of the traits of a confident person
- Breakdown of the traits of a socially awkward person
- Easy, actionable tips for overcoming being socially awkward
- Confidence checklist to ensure you're on the right path of self-development

To grab your free bonus book just tap here, or go to:

https://theartofmastery.com/confidence/

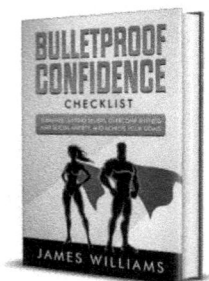

Introduction

Congratulations on purchasing *Social Anxiety* and thank you for doing so.

The following chapters will discuss what social anxiety and shyness are and give you strategies to manage your social anxiety and shyness.

Despite being very similar, the conditions are different from one another. In the first section of this book, we will look at the psychology of how they are different and where they come from. The similarities between the two conditions will be examined, and the process the brain goes through when the feelings of shyness and social anxiety flare up.

The second section will offer tips, tools, and strategies to prevent social anxiety- related panic and manage shyness in a social situation. These strategies may be different from what you've read before, but they are all simple and easy to adjust in your daily life.

You have probably read other books and visited websites to find help for your shyness and maybe you have asked professionals for insight. You have probably reached the point that feeling awkward and tense around others means you begin to avoid social situations. Have you ever had your mind go blank in the face of talking to new people? Do you have a hard time making lasting, meaningful relationships? This book will help you find out *why* you feel this way and *how* to manage the feelings.

There are plenty of books on this subject on the market. Thanks again for choosing this one! Every effort was made to ensure it is full of as much useful information as possible. Please enjoy!

Chapter 1: Social Anxiety and Shyness Explained

Social anxiety and shyness are both psychological misfires in the brain, but social anxiety goes deeper than shyness. Social anxiety is the fear of being judged in a negative way by others, while shyness is a feeling of being awkward or tense around others. Both have a root cause of fear - fear of being judged, a fear of saying the wrong things, but they each come from very different parts of the mind.

Social Anxiety Disorder means that the person experiencing it has such fear of social situations that they either suffer through them with a high level of strain on their emotions or avoid social situations entirely. They experience deep fear of being humiliated or judged for anything they may say or do, or even what they wear. While some people who suffer from social anxiety are shy, it is not the case with everyone. Statistics show that only approximately 50% of people who have social anxiety claim to be shy. Oftentimes, people with social anxiety want to participate and be able to talk and have lasting, meaningful relationships, but their fear of humiliation and thoughts of anxiety inhibit their ability. They also feel very negatively toward their anxious feelings, continually mentally berating themselves when they experience their symptoms. Living with social anxiety can also mean other mental disorders as well, such as depression, drugs or alcohol addiction, and eating disorders.

Shyness is actually considered a character trait. Most people who are shy do not consider it a bad thing about themselves. These people do experience anxiety and worry about saying or doing the wrong things, but while it does inhibit their behavior somewhat, they are able to maintain a steady mood without the loop of irrational and negative thoughts. Shy people tend to get past their social concerns once they become more familiar with their surroundings. While being shy is not the same as social anxiety, shyness can evolve into social anxiety under the right conditions. Allowing your shyness to keep you from joining in on new things, letting your focus fall on thinking negative, and withdrawing from your circle of friends nurtures the conditions under which you will begin suffering from social anxiety. Additionally, having unrealistic expectations or drawing irrational conclusions about an upcoming event could exacerbate your shyness and transform it into social anxiety. Going into a situation expecting to be rejected or focusing too intensely on your anxious reaction will only serve to make it a self-fulfilling prophecy, and a feeling of failure afterward.

Biologically speaking, social anxiety was necessary for prehistoric days when living outside of a tribe meant essentially, death. In the civilizations where everyone contributed their skills and were a part of a tribe's culture for hunting, gathering, and homesteading, being "strange" or "too quiet" meant that a person was often avoided or even cast out of a tribe. Being conscious of one's thoughts, actions, and words were important in keeping one's tribe. Tribes also had to be able to communicate with one another in order to grow and not die out, so they had to be aware of what would make members of other tribes shun them. Therefore, it makes sense that social anxiety has prehistoric roots, because of those roots and the amount of time it takes to evolve traits in humans, social anxiety, and shyness are an inherent part of our genetics.

The feelings we get of anxiety or shyness in new or stressful situations is set off by what's called the "fight or flight" response - the intuitive reaction your mind automatically engages when you are faced with scary situations. The "fight" response makes you want to stand your ground and face down what is in front of you. The "flight" response makes you want to remove yourself from the situation immediately so as to avoid the inevitable danger that set off the response. For most people, this response is programmed properly and does not activate during innocuous situations such as a new study group or, say, a blind date. However, in some cases, the fight or flight is set off in the face of these same situations.

These are not feelings that you can just force down. It's something that you have to work on to retrain your brain to recognize the anxious signals and head off the automatic fear response. Your mind's reflex is to react adversely when you are confronted with a situation that makes you uncomfortable socially. In order to be able to overcome what is holding you back, you have to first become aware of what is triggering the reaction, then work to mitigate the negativity associated with it.

When someone makes statements like, "Don't overthink it" or "Don't be silly, you're fine!", or even, "It's all in your head. You don't have anything to worry about," you can pretty well know that they have not experienced shyness or social anxiety. They don't understand how hard it is for you to simply show up to a gathering and keep an expression besides abject fear or unyielding stress on your face. They don't comprehend how courageous you are just to be out there, facing the fear that makes your mind reflexively try to fight or flee.

There are also cases of a chemical imbalance in the brain. The chemical in the brain called, *serotonin,* manages the regulation of moods and emotional reaction. In cases of social anxiety, the production of serotonin in the brain has been found to be either dampened or grossly underproduced. This causes the irrational feelings of nervousness and fear, as well as making it difficult to come out of those feelings without conscious effort. While an underproduction of a brain chemical is a physiological matter, you can use psychological efforts to boost this level with some practice.

While there are medications available to treat social anxiety, they are only meant to be temporary solutions, and sometimes there is not a good fit between you and the medication (meaning, it doesn't work), or the side effects are worse than the ailment the medication is treating. Some people simply do not want to take prescription medication. A physiological reaction may be the cause of your anxiety or shyness, but that does not mean that the only solution is pharmaceutical drugs. In the next section, we will discuss natural and sustainable ways to overcome and manage your social anxiety or shyness.

Don't let this get you down, though. Even though social anxiety and shyness are part of our genes, that doesn't necessarily mean that we're doomed to stay stuck with these conditions that don't serve such a dire purpose in modern times. Our genetics determine how our bodies and minds react in situations based on past experiences and what our adult guardians taught us growing up.

Fortunately, your mind is adaptable and once you get down to the bottom of what causes your anxiety and shyness, you can work through those things and overcome the problem.

In order to get to the root of your fear, you first have to become aware of it and how it begins. Does the thought of meeting new people make you sweat? Do you become quiet or say awkward things in a group? Is it difficult for you to hold a conversation?

What happens in your mind when you are facing a situation that normally makes you feel shy? What is the first thought that springs up? If you are worried that you won't be able to hold a conversation, think about why that is. Your past experiences are what shape your current thoughts, so there is something possibly in your unconscious mind that makes you think you can't hold a conversation. Even if you can't immediately come up with the *why*, you can become aware of your thoughts when your anxiety starts and work back from there.

You may experience physical side effects of anxiety and shyness. Aside from the sweaty palms and racing thoughts, you likely have a hard time not only thinking of things to say but actually going through to form the words and engage your voice. You get tongue-tied. Then, your cycle of negative thoughts and feelings become compounded by this negative experience, leading to more anxiety and a harder time overcoming the anxiety in the next social situation you face.

Thoughts are not initially negative or positive, just like social anxiety doesn't come out of anywhere. However, it is the emotion brought on by the thought that is designated negative or positive, and that emotion is a conditioned response from previous experiences, either from your own personal experience, or the experience of a trusted person in your life. When your mind recognizes the negative emotion attached to the thought of social situations, it begins the cycle of negative thoughts. When thoughts occur in the brain, they have to find a neuron to travel down to appear in your working mind. If that neuron has a negative connotation to it, you are more likely to experience anxiety, fear, or sadness associated with that thought.

Here is where shyness and social anxiety differ. A shy person may experience a slightly elevated heart rate, and some worry about if their hair is in place. Whereas a person with social anxiety experiences sweating, a notable increase in heart rate, a feeling of not being good enough, and a solid fear that everything they say or do will garner a negative reaction. Feelings of shyness generally lessen after a time of being in a social situation; however, a person with social anxiety will not get relief from their fears until the social stimulation is gone.

A shy person probably comes from a family of at least one or two people that are shy and nervous. Someone suffering social anxiety is running off the memory of frequently overexaggerated-rejection and extreme social awkwardness. Social anxiety is learned, while shyness is a part of someone's personality.

Shyness and social anxiety have some repercussions that may affect a person's life. If you have social anxiety, you probably avoid most social situations if possible because you know it will cause you a high amount of stress. If you do attend, you stay off to the side and don't talk to anyone because you feel like no one would want to talk to you or they would think you are strange. A shy person could miss out on an opportunity to network for their job or meet that special someone because their nerves didn't dissipate quickly enough to act. A person with social anxiety might have those same missed opportunities but would put themselves through a mental lashing for not being able to go after them due to their anxiety.

Depression can also be caused by social anxiety and shyness. Since a part of social anxiety is avoidance of social situations, it instigates isolation. When you are isolated, you are staying away from the friends and family who can help you come out of the cycle of negativity and sadness. You are limiting your opportunities not only to make more memories and friends but also practice the many ways to overcome your fears. Your quality of life is affected in ways that seem small but could actually have larger consequences than you realize.

Think about it - if you are shy, you are less likely to approach people. If you can't talk to people, meeting a new friend or special someone is difficult. Approaching your boss for a raise or promotion is not as probable to happen if you are shy. You will not branch out your social network, which means you miss out on adventures and stories that your other friends have (along with a richer quality of life.) You could miss out on the opportunity to become a valuable employee and earn more money. If you are shy in school, you have more of a probability of poor school performance simply because you can't manage your anxiety. Poor performance in school has a lasting lifetime effect on your life.

Shyness and social anxiety inhibit your best self. If you have tried other advice and still find that you have more shyness or social anxiety than you'd like, you will want to read the next section to see how to identify what begins your shyness and anxiety, as well as ways to manage them or beat those feelings altogether.

Chapter 2: Shyness and Social Anxiety Managed

There are many ways in which overcoming and managing your social anxiety and shyness can be mapped. Most experts agree that Cognitive Behavioral Therapy is a good place to start, but there are other, smaller things that you can do in your daily life to make adjustments that will relieve your feelings.

As stated in the previous section, in order to master your anxiety, you first have to find where it comes from. What was it in your past that started to make you feel as though you were not good enough, smart enough, and cool enough to be in public around people? Did you have a presentation at school that didn't go as you'd like? Was it that time you asked out your middle school sweetheart and she said no? There is some triggering event for your social anxiety that needs to be uncovered so that you can examine it and work through it.

That being said, shyness may not have that same type of initiation. Maybe you've always been the quiet kid or the kid who blushes when girls talk to you. Where people with social anxiety have a starting point, people who are shy tend to be born that way or encouraged to be quiet as a young child. Knowing the difference between the two conditions as well as being able to differentiate which you suffer from, is key to learning best how to cope since they have different starting points.

Although, the conditions sometimes do overlap, as in the case of symptoms and physical expression. Both have symptoms of sweating, not being able to think clearly, higher heart rate, blushing, and trembling. If you can't use the prevention tools that will be discussed, there will also be a section for management or stopping the symptoms when they happen. Both conditions also have a knee-jerk reaction of retreat or avoid, which will be discussed also.

However, while they are similar in some respects, they are different in others. Sometimes treatment for shyness is different than the treatment for social anxiety, which can be more involved than shyness. We will discuss strategies that will work for both social anxiety and shyness, then more specific strategies for social anxiety and shyness.

A good place to start getting over either shyness or anxiety is being mindful. Staying aware of where you are, what is going on around you, and keeping your focus on the person talking to you will help distract your mind from its anxious thoughts. If the forefront of your mind is staying in the present and actively listening to what your conversation partner is saying, it is easier to keep the conversation going. The bonus here is the person you are talking to will feel like you really are interested in what they have to say. Imagine how handy that will be when you are talking to potential romantic partners! By keeping your mind and focus on them and not zoning out, trying to come up with your responses, and looking them in the eye, you are communicating to them that they are important to you. Moreover, what love interest doesn't want to feel important and cherished by their significant other? The intrinsic (inner self) bonus is that you will be able to talk and concentrate without letting the fears and concerns rob you of the here and now when you are most wanting to be present. Your anxiety and shyness are, essentially, drowned out. You will be able to enjoy your friends and be there for their actions so that you can be a part of the story and not someone who had to hear it second hand. Imagine how great it would be, the potential memories you will make when you are fully present and not worried about what's happening in your head. Being mindful is a great step toward overcoming the shyness and anxiety that is holding you back while being just a small daily adjustment you make in your mind.

Self-help manuals can also help if there are a clear and easy-to-follow premise and relevant exercises for you to do. Obviously, the manuals you have read up to this point have not done what you needed of them, so maybe it's time to try some external, physical, and visible work. Get a manual from a reputable psychiatrist or group. Usually, books from university psychology professors are very helpful, because many of the strategies and thought processes they write about are things they see every day, if not employ themselves. They are reading (and assigning!) case study after case study, analyzing them, interpreting them, and are able to see the scientific data that backs up what their book is claiming. If you flip through a book and can't tell what the author is trying to help you do, it is probably not a reputable (or effective) book, so move on. Sometimes self-help manuals are used in conjunction with therapy, but for the purpose of this book, a good self-help manual is something you can take 10 to 15 minutes each day to read from and put the advice into action. Keep in mind, though, that self-help books only work if you follow their directions, whether or not you feel the author is credible. If you choose this route, be prepared for using self-motivation to stick with it. Of course, you have already come across something that motivated you to read this book, so that shouldn't be too much of a problem with the right book.

Talking seems like it might be counterproductive as a legitimate way to address shyness and social anxiety since it means talking to a person, (technically, a social situation), but it is usually more cathartic to share your burdens with someone else. You don't have to tell them every detail of your day or experience unless you just want to. The purpose of talking isn't to raise your anxiety or shyness, but instead, help manage the feeling that spring up when you are in situations that make you uncomfortable. Talk with someone who knows you, and who you can trust not to make you feel bad about your experiences. This way, you will have someone there you know you can trust, while you practice getting a handle on the physical symptoms you experience when your shyness or anxiety flares up. This is very helpful simply because when you talk to someone who understands how you feel, you don't feel so isolated in your thoughts and feelings. You are not keeping toxic feelings and information inside your body but putting it out into the open so that you don't feel like you are carrying the weight of the world and maybe getting some legitimately helpful advice. Talking is a simple, effective action that can help you overcome your anxieties.

Practice confidence in yourself and pay attention to how it makes you feel on the inside. Sure, you might have to fake it at first out in public, but, hey, you're out in public. You didn't let your anxiety keep you locked away in your house. That in itself should be a good confidence boost since you have already proved to yourself that you are capable of setting aside your concerns. Once you have something positive to build on, authentic confidence becomes easier to achieve. When you walk, don't stare at the ground. When you talk, use a clear voice. Make eye contact with people to show them that you are important. If you help yourself feel important, that feeling will grow with the more you are able to do it. Positive behavior can be just as easy as negative behavior once you practice enough.

Journaling, or simply writing down your day, can be extremely effective in helping you become more aware of your feelings before, during, and after social situations. That will help you learn what your triggers are so that you can either become more comfortable in the situations where they come up or work around them so that you don't have to face them and allow the anxiety to spark. It doesn't have to be drawn out, or something that you do each and every time you have a feeling of anxiety or shyness, but just 10-

15 minutes a day spent reflecting on what happened during that day will be almost as effective as talking to someone without the fear of them judging you if you really, truly feel that you have no one you can talk to.

Treatment for social anxiety apart from shyness is different than trying to overcome both conditions. Sometimes you are socially anxious in situations where you would enjoy being an active participant rather than a passive bystander - that is not you being shy, that is the negative thoughts and feelings that cause your anxiety taking up the forefront of your mind. In light of this, some more in-depth treatment may be necessary.

When learning how to manage social anxiety, one good way to get started on conquering it is through trying things out of your comfort zone. Consider where you are comfortable: are you ok poolside with two close friends? Can you handle a party as long as you know the host? Once you figure out your limit, consider what the next step would be. Could you hang out at the pool with someone whom you don't know, as well as the two friends you normally hang out with? Try it. Stay present and be focused on what's happening around you. Try going to a birthday celebration at a restaurant for a co-worker. Try little new things to expand your comfort zone and help you face your fears. Conversely, never stepping outside your zone can make it shrink, which will only make the social anxiety worse - the opposite of your goal. Sure, you will be uncomfortable, but that's the point. You are working toward expanding the scope you are currently living in. If you never try something uncomfortable, can you really say that you've done all you can to get over your condition?

Social anxiety is often triggered by an initial thought, which then attaches to a memory and subsequent emotion. Part of treating social anxiety is tracking down that thought and that memory. The memory that supports a thought as negative is most often hidden behind the anxiety, which understandably makes it difficult to see and work through it. Stick it out and find out what sparks your anxiety. Were you bullied as a kid and now you fear being picked on again? Did you enter the science fair with an amazing project including demonstration and didn't win? After tracking down and working through the negative memory, you may even find that the memory you had was flawed and blown out of proportion. Understanding where your negative thought comes from will enable you to remind yourself that the memory is flawed, and you can let the feeling of anxiety go without having a physical reaction to it. Doing this requires you to be aware of what is on your mind when your anxious thoughts begin. When you recognize the signs of impending social anxiety, you can avoid the anxiety from spinning out of control because you are able to reign in your mind before it gets out of control.

Take stock of what matters. You are a valuable, brave person with a lot to offer. In the grand scheme of things, people are mostly wrapped up in their own problems and don't have time to worry about if your shirt is tucked or untucked. Ask yourself if the judgment of others is practical when the apocalypse starts. After all, you're the one with the safe bunker and everyone else just wants a corner of it.

Confront your negative feelings. Ask yourself, "Is this response realistic or do I need a reality check?" "Does it hurt anyone if I show up like this?" or "Is there a parachute nearby so that I can bail if I need it?" Is it possible that you are only projecting that there will be a disaster? By questioning your feelings, you are making yourself think from another, more grounded perspective, which allows you to come back to the present reality.

If you feel that you don't have social anxiety, but you are shy and want to change that about yourself, there are some small things you can do as well.

The old saying "fake it 'til you make it" is still offered as advice today for a reason. Training your mind to lean into a more positive mindset is made easier when you are already portraying yourself as confident. You already know what it looks like to be confident, and even though you might fake your confidence at first, your brain will become attuned to how you are acting and can move easily into that feeling in a more genuine way. Your mind starts to acclimate itself to the outward appearance and if you can go into a situation believing it will go well, you will be looking for the openings to make the situation feel better for you instead of focusing on how awkward you feel.

Watch the self- criticism. As a shy person, you tend to be harder on yourself for not participating more or being as "normal" like your best friend than you would be if you were not shy. This also leads to lower self-esteem and a higher risk of depression. Be mindful of the way you talk to yourself. Would you talk to your mother that way? If not, then it's not nice enough to say to yourself. Don't make the mistake of undervaluing yourself or everyone will think it's okay to capitalize on your lack of self-worth. If it's not sweet to say it about your mother, then it's not acceptable to be negative about yourself.

Don't call attention to your shyness, either. First, it sets you up with any new people around you to try and take advantage of you being shy. Broadcasting that you are shy is equivalent to wearing "I'm insecure" on a sandwich board in the middle of Times Square. Calling yourself out gives the expectation that you will say something awkward and the people around you would have an excuse for avoiding you. Second, pointing out that you are shy can lead people to expect that you will say or do something that doesn't present well with your actual self. Many times, shyness is overwhelming in your mind but not visible on the outside, or, at least, so mild that the new person in your group may never even notice.

These are just a couple of ways to manage or control your social anxiety. Start with these tips and move to more detailed ones if you find that you are still too shy or too anxious in social settings than you would like to be. There are many resources available to help with both social anxiety and shyness, including workbooks and effective exercises that work on getting you out into the world.

Conclusion:

Thank for making it through to the end of *Social Anxiety*. Let's hope it was informative and able to provide you with all of the tools you need to achieve your goals of being free from shyness and social anxiety.

The next step is to get out there and practice. Use the starting points in Chapter 2 to help you beat your anxiety or shyness. You know the *why* of social anxiety and shyness and the *how* of getting past the feelings. Now it's time to put them to use. Social anxiety and shyness do not mean you can't lead a full, rich life. You can beat the challenges presented by social anxiety and shyness.

Thank you!

Before you go, I just wanted to say thank you for purchasing my book.

You could have picked from dozens of other books on the same topic but you took a chance and chose this one.

So, a HUGE thanks to you for getting this book and for reading all the way to the end.

Now I wanted to ask you for a small favor. **Could you please consider posting a review on the platform? Reviews are one of the easiest ways to support the work of independent authors.**

This feedback will help me continue to write the type of books that will help you get the results you want. So if you enjoyed it, please let me know! (-:

Lastly, don't forget to grab a copy of your Free Bonus book *"Bulletproof Confidence Checklist"*.

If you want to learn how to overcome shyness and social anxiety and become more confident then this book is for you.

Just go to:

<u>https://theartofmastery.com/confidence/</u>